Francis Frith's

Around
Newport

Photographic Memories

Francis Frith's

Around
Newport

Louise Tolcher

FRITH
BOOK Co

First published in the United Kingdom in 2001 by
Frith Book Company Ltd

Paperback Edition 2001
ISBN 1-85937-258-9

Hardback Edition 2001
ISBN 1-85937-362-3

British Library Cataloguing in Publication Data

Francis Frith's Newport
Louise Tolcher

Frith Book Company Ltd
Frith's Barn, Teffont,
Salisbury, Wiltshire SP3 5QP
Tel: +44 (0) 1722 716 376
Email: info@frithbook.co.uk
www.frithbook.co.uk

Printed and bound in Great Britain

Front Cover: Commercial Street 1901 47896

Contents

Francis Frith: *Victorian Pioneer*

FRANCIS FRITH, Victorian founder of the world-famous photographic archive, was a complex and multi-talented man. A devout Quaker and a highly successful Victorian businessman, he was both philosophic by nature and pioneering in outlook.

By 1855 Francis Frith had already established a wholesale grocery business in Liverpool, and sold it for the astonishing sum of £200,000, which is the equivalent today of over £15,000,000. Now a multi-millionaire, he was able to indulge his passion for travel. As a child he had pored over travel books written by early explorers, and his fancy and imagination had been stirred by family holidays to the sublime mountain regions of Wales and Scotland. 'What a land of spirit-stirring and enriching scenes and places!' he had written. He was to return to these scenes of grandeur in later years to 'recapture the thousands of vivid and tender memories', but with a different purpose. Now in his thirties, and captivated by the new science of photography, Frith set out on a series of pioneering journeys to the Nile regions that occupied him from 1856 until 1860.

Intrigue and Adventure

He took with him on his travels a specially-designed wicker carriage that acted as both dark-room and sleeping chamber. These far-flung journeys were packed with intrigue and adventure. In his life story, written when he was sixty-three, Frith tells of being held captive by bandits, and of fighting 'an awful midnight battle to the very point of surrender with a deadly pack of hungry, wild dogs'. Sporting flowing Arab costume, Frith arrived at Akaba by camel seventy years before Lawrence, where he encountered 'desert princes and rival sheikhs, blazing with jewel-hilted swords'.

During these extraordinary adventures he was assiduously exploring the desert regions bordering the Nile and patiently recording the antiquities and peoples with his camera. He was the first photographer to venture beyond the sixth cataract. Africa was still the mysterious 'Dark Continent', and Stanley and Livingstone's historic meeting was a decade into the future. The conditions for picture taking confound belief. He laboured for hours in his wicker dark-room in the sweltering heat of the desert, while the volatile chemicals fizzed dangerously in their trays. Often he was forced to work in remote tombs and caves where conditions were cooler. Back in London he exhibited his photographs and was 'rapturously cheered' by members of the Royal Society. His reputation as a

photographer was made overnight. An eminent modern historian has likened their impact on the population of the time to that on our own generation of the first photographs taken on the surface of the moon.

Venture of a Life-Time

Characteristically, Frith quickly spotted the opportunity to create a new business as a specialist publisher of photographs. He lived in an era of immense and sometimes violent change. For the poor in the early part of Victoria's reign work was a drudge and the hours long, and people had precious little free time to enjoy themselves. Most had no transport other than a cart or gig at their disposal, and had not travelled far beyond the boundaries of their own town or village. However,

by the 1870s, the railways had threaded their way across the country, and Bank Holidays and half-day Saturdays had been made obligatory by Act of Parliament. All of a sudden the ordinary working man and his family were able to enjoy days out and see a little more of the world.

With characteristic business acumen, Francis Frith foresaw that these new tourists would enjoy having souvenirs to commemorate their days out. In 1860 he married Mary Ann Rosling and set out with the intention of photographing every city, town and village in Britain. For the next thirty years he travelled the country by train and by pony and trap, producing fine photographs of seaside resorts and beauty spots that were keenly bought by millions of Victorians. These prints were painstakingly pasted into family albums and pored over during the dark nights of winter, rekindling precious memories of summer excursions.

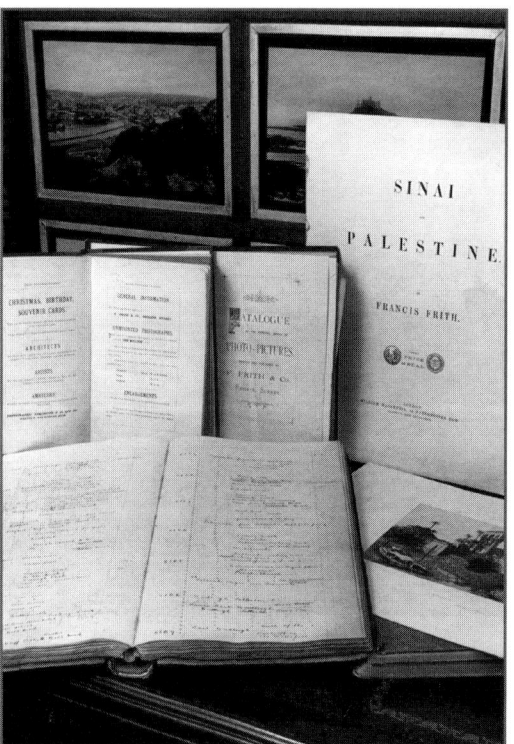

The Rise of Frith & Co

Frith's studio was soon supplying retail shops all over the country. To meet the demand he gathered about him a small team of photographers, and published the work of independent artist-photographers of the calibre of Roger Fenton and Francis Bedford. In order to gain some understanding of the scale of Frith's business one only has to look at the catalogue issued by Frith & Co in 1886: it runs to some 670 pages, listing not only many thousands of views of the British Isles but also many photographs of most European countries, and China, Japan, the USA and Canada – note the sample page shown above from the hand-written *Frith & Co* ledgers detailing pictures taken. By 1890 Frith had created the greatest specialist photographic publishing company in the world,

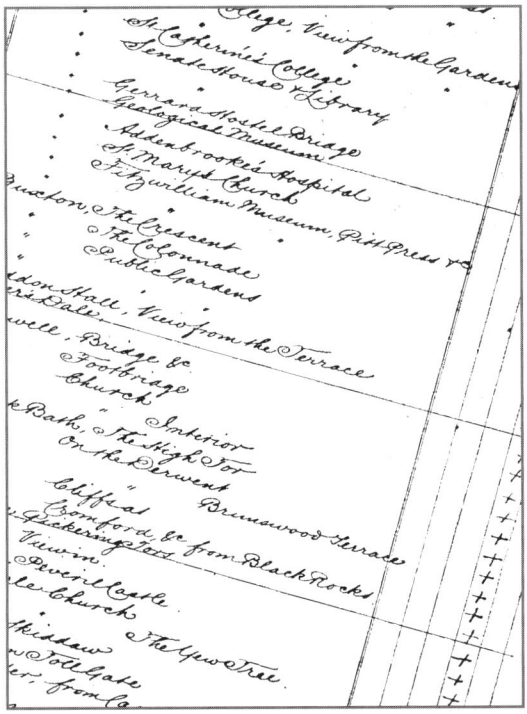

Frith's death, a new card measuring 5.5 x 3.5 inches became the standard format, but it was not until 1902 that the divided back came into being, with address and message on one face and a full-size illustration on the other. *Frith & Co* were in the vanguard of postcard development, and Frith's sons Eustace and Cyril continued their father's monumental task, expanding the number of views offered to the public and recording more and more places in Britain, as the coasts and countryside were opened up to mass travel.

Francis Frith died in 1898 at his villa in Cannes, his great project still growing. The archive he created continued in business for another seventy years. By 1970 it contained over a third of a million pictures of 7,000 cities, towns and villages. The massive photographic record Frith has left to us stands as a living monument to a special and very remarkable man.

with over 2,000 outlets – more than the combined number that Boots and W H Smith have today! The picture on the right shows the *Frith & Co* display board at Ingleton in the Yorkshire Dales. Beautifully constructed with mahogany frame and gilt inserts, it could display up to a dozen local scenes.

Postcard Bonanza

The ever-popular holiday postcard we know today took many years to develop. In 1870 the Post Office issued the first plain cards, with a pre-printed stamp on one face. In 1894 they allowed other publishers' cards to be sent through the mail with an attached adhesive halfpenny stamp. Demand grew rapidly, and in 1895 a new size of postcard was permitted called the court card, but there was little room for illustration. In 1899, a year after

Frith's Archive: *A Unique Legacy*

FRANCIS FRITH'S legacy to us today is of immense significance and value, for the magnificent archive of evocative photographs he created provides a unique record of change in 7,000 cities, towns and villages throughout Britain over a century and more. Frith and his fellow studio photographers revisited locations many times down the years to update their views, compiling for us an enthralling and colourful pageant of British life and character.

We tend to think of Frith's sepia views of Britain as nostalgic, for most of us use them to conjure up memories of places in our own lives with which we have family associations. It often makes us forget that to Francis Frith they were records of daily life as it was actually being lived in the cities, towns and villages of his day. The Victorian age was one of great and often bewildering change for ordinary people, and though the pictures evoke an impression of slower times, life was as busy and hectic as it is today.

We are fortunate that Frith was a photographer of the people, dedicated to recording the minutiae of everyday life. For it is this sheer wealth of visual data, the painstaking chronicle of changes in dress, transport, street layouts, buildings, housing, engineering and landscape that captivates us so much today. His remarkable images offer us a powerful link with the past and with the lives of our ancestors.

Today's Technology

Computers have now made it possible for Frith's many thousands of images to be accessed almost instantly. In the Frith archive today, each photograph is carefully 'digitised' then stored on a CD Rom. Frith archivists can locate a single photograph amongst thousands within seconds. Views can be catalogued and sorted under a variety of categories of place and content to the immediate benefit of researchers.

Inexpensive reference prints can be created for them at the touch of a mouse button, and a wide range of books and other printed materials assembled and published for a wider, more general readership - in the next twelve months over a hundred Frith local history titles will be published! The day-to-day workings of the archive are very different from how they were in Francis Frith's time: imagine the herculean task of sorting through eleven tons of glass negatives as Frith had to do to locate a particular sequence of pictures! Yet

See Frith at www. frithbook.co.uk

the archive still prides itself on maintaining the same high standards of excellence laid down by Francis Frith, including the painstaking cataloguing and indexing of every view.

It is curious to reflect on how the internet now allows researchers in America and elsewhere greater instant access to the archive than Frith himself ever enjoyed. Many thousands of individual views can be called up on screen within seconds on one of the Frith internet sites, enabling people living continents away to revisit the streets of their ancestral home town, or view places in Britain where they have enjoyed holidays. Many overseas researchers welcome the chance to view special theme selections, such as transport, sports, costume and ancient monuments.

We are certain that Francis Frith would have heartily approved of these modern developments in imaging techniques, for he himself was always working at the very limits of Victorian photographic technology.

The Value of the Archive Today

Because of the benefits brought by the computer, Frith's images are increasingly studied by social historians, by researchers into genealogy and ancestory, by architects, town planners, and by teachers and schoolchildren involved in local history projects.

In addition, the archive offers every one of us an opportunity to examine the places where we and our families have lived and worked down the years. Highly successful in Frith's own era, the archive is now, a century and more on, entering a new phase of popularity.

The Past in Tune with the Future

Historians consider the Francis Frith Collection to be of prime national importance. It is the only archive of its kind remaining in private ownership and has been valued at a million pounds. However, this figure is now rapidly increasing as digital technology enables more and more people around the world to enjoy its benefits.

Francis Frith's archive is now housed in an historic timber barn in the beautiful village of Teffont in Wiltshire. Its founder would not recognize the archive office as it is today. In place of the many thousands of dusty boxes containing glass plate negatives and an all-pervading odour of photographic chemicals, there are now ranks of computer screens. He would be amazed to watch his images travelling round the world at unimaginable speeds through network and internet lines.

The archive's future is both bright and exciting. Francis Frith, with his unshakeable belief in making photographs available to the greatest number of people, would undoubtedly approve of what is being done today with his lifetime's work. His photographs, depicting our shared past, are now bringing pleasure and enlightenment to millions around the world a century and more after his death.

Newport - *Casnewydd*

Casnewydd is a contraction of Castell-Newydd-Ar-Wysg, which means 'a new castle upon the Usk'.

'TERRA MARIQUE', MEANING 'by land and sea', is the motto on Newport's coat of arms. Both land and sea have contributed to the invasion and domination of this area by outlanders. More importantly, they have contributed to her progression to a successful industrial town.

Initially, a Celtic tribe called the Silures, who came from Europe, occupied Newport. The arrival of the Romans under Emperor Claudius in AD43 loosened the Silures' hold over South Wales, which eventually succumbed to Roman rule in AD90. A garrison town was constructed at Caerleon to maintain this control. Three centuries later, the Romans abandoned Britain and left us vulnerable and open to attack. The Danes invaded in the 11th century, and were followed by Harold six years before his death at the Battle of Hastings.

Newport began to grow as a town in the early 13th century, when Newport castle was rebuilt in stone. At this time walls encircled it with north, east and west gates. Development was halted by Owain Glyndwr's invasion of Monmouthshire, which had long been a buffer state between England and Wales and thus endured frequent battles. Newport, both castle and town, was destroyed in 1402, and was said to be so ravaged as to be worth nothing.

A century later, owing to the Act of Union between England and Wales, the county of Monmouthshire was formed; in 1623, Newport's status increased with the granting of a Royal Charter. This resulted in the appointment of a mayor and councillors to preside over Newport's affairs.

The beginning of the 1800s saw Newport with a population of just over a thousand. The town consisted of the area surrounding the castle and the bridge down to the Westgate, and from the base of the High Street upward via Church Street, now Stow Hill, to St Woolos. At this time Newport boasted a small but superior harbour, capable of housing small vessels. It soon became evident that improvements in her shipping facilities were needed, as the majority of South Wales coal was exported from here. Newport Docks is situated where the rivers Ebbw and Usk meet - the depth of the Usk is advantageous. The Industrial Revolution had taken a hold on Newport. The opening of the Monmouthshire and Brecon canal in 1799 influenced this, as rich mineral resources could be exploited. Coal and iron could be delivered to Newport Docks for shipment; most of the coal went to Bristol and Bridgwater. By the end of the 19th century, the railways had replaced the canals as the main haulier of Newport's industrial goods.

In 1842 the new Town Dock was opened; it was situated between Newport and George Street Bridge, and covered an area of four acres. An extension was completed sixteen years later. The completion of the dock was accompanied by much celebration, and a carnival atmosphere existed within the town. With prosperity comes money, money that could be used on leisure time. The gangs of navvies who worked on the docks certainly took advantage of this. Around this time Newport had a population of about 14,000, and for every 39 inhabitants there was at least one public house. As further testament to industrial growth, in 1875 Mrs Benjamin Evans opened Alexandra Dock after it had been seven years in construction, and South Alexandra Dock was opened in 1893. During its extensions in 1909, there was a disaster that killed thirty-three men. From the tragedy there emerged a boy hero named Tom (Toya) Lewis, who was presented with the Albert Medal.

We might think that in these years of rejuvenation, the workers of South Wales would be content and enjoying a percentage of the growing wealth and better social conditions; but unfortunately this was not so. The Chartist movement hoped to form a new government that would ease the many hardships of working men and women. Chartism was named after the People's Charter, a list of aims meant to alleviate their oppression: a vote for all men in elections, an equal number of people to vote in each district, people should vote in a secret ballot, MPs to be elected every year, men need not be property owners to become members of Parliament, and Members of

Parliament should be paid a salary. In 1839 the Chartist riots took place. Zephaniah Williams, William Jones and Newport-born ex-mayor John Frost each led a group of working men on a march into Newport. They convened on the Westgate hotel; here soldiers waited, shots were fired and a riot took place. Twenty people were killed. John Frost was arrested and exiled. He returned to Newport in 1856, and lived to the grand age of ninety-three. John Frost Square in the heart of Newport's town centre, complete with a large mosaic, pays tribute to him.

Further unrest developed during the depression which swept the nation in the 1930s. Unemployment was higher here than anywhere in Britain. The changes in world markets meant that Newport's coal exports were halved and the Town Dock was closed in 1931. Fifty years on, Newport was trading in fruit and timber. Llanwern Steelworks were opened in 1962 by Her Majesty Queen Elizabeth II. The immense three and a half miles-long works offered hope and thousands of jobs. Once owned by the state and known as The British Steel Corporation, it is now run by Corus, and its future is very uncertain.

Aside from its industry, Newport has always embraced its recreational and leisure time, with religion, of course, playing a great part. Newport must be a typical Welsh town, for it has been said that even in the smallest town in Wales, you are guaranteed to find a church and a pub. Newport's

origins can be linked with its most famous church and landmark, St Woolos Cathedral. Its founder, St Gwynllyw, was the warrior leader of the ancient kingdom of Margannwg. Owain Glyndwr and later Harold sacked it, and from here the Chartists marched past down Stow Hill into Newport. Entertainment was provided for the inhabitants of Newport by theatres such as the Lyceum, which started life as the Victoria Hall in 1863, positioned on the corner of Bridge and Station Streets. Harry Houdini played here twice; it was converted to a cinema in 1929, and finally demolished in 1961. Other theatres included the Gaiety, the Theatre Royal, the Empire Palace, the New Theatre and (still a popular choice today) the Dolman Theatre.

Art and culture were enhanced in 1888 by the opening of Newport Museum and Art Gallery, which in 1968 moved to its current position in John Frost Square; it also now incorporates a substantial library. In recent years, Newport County Borough has commissioned a number of public works. In 1991 they uncovered a statue commemorating the Chartist riots in Westgate Square, a memorial in honour of the Merchant Navy was erected at the junction of Kingsway and Cardiff road, and lastly, 'The Wave' by Peter Fink, a giant steel sculpture meant to reflect Newport's maritime heritage was set up. In 1990 a statue was unveiled in Commercial Street of Newport's 'tramp poet', W H Davies. William Henry Davies was born at the centre of a seafaring community in Portland Street,

Pillgwenlly on 3 July 1871: he is best remembered for his 'Autobiography of a Supertramp'. His poems were filled with images of Newport. In 'Love Absent' he wrote:

> The banks of Alteryn are now less sweet,
> Nor Malpas brook more chary of his flower,
> And I unchanged as they…..

Regular concerts are held at Newport Centre, a sports and leisure complex opened in 1985 by Neil Kinnock. The Kings Hotel continues to offer a menu of blues, swing and rock and roll - Van Morrison is just one of its famous performers. T J's night-club in Clarence Place presents a more contemporary bill. Its shabby exterior hides a popular and successful platform for both established and up-and-coming musicians. On visiting Newport one

attraction that should not be missed is Tradegar House. This beautiful 17th-century house was for 500 years the ancestral home of the Morgan family. Following Lord Tradegar's departure in 1951, it was converted into a school. Newport Borough Council initiated an intense restoration programme in the 1970s. Today the public can visit its exquisite interiors and impressive grounds, and it also holds tours, exhibitions, plays and concerts.

As we walk through Newport, it is advisable to look up so as to be able to appreciate the Georgian and Victorian architecture that remains in the town. Its accelerated development during the Industrial Revolution and the years following it, which aimed at turning the town into a city, unfortunately ravaged the town's skyline - this all in the name of progress. Newport continues to be a melting pot of style and taste, a mixture of industry and beautiful

The Origins of Newport

Romans & Religion

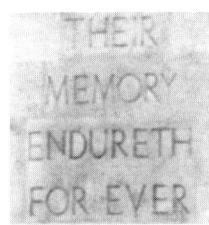

St Woolos Church 1899 43663
This beautiful, essentially 12th-century church was originally dedicated to St Gwynllyw, a 5th-century warrior saint, who built the first church on this site, and is now buried here. The name was transformed through the years by changes in Latin and Welsh to eventually become St Woolos. In the foreground we can see part of the churchyard where ten Chartist marchers lie, in an unmarked grave; a stone plaque near the main entrance honours them.

St Woolos Church 1893 32632
We stand here looking down Stow Hill, the imposing structure of the church's tower dominating our view. Jasper Tudor, Duke of Bedford and uncle of Henry VII, constructed this 15th-century bastion, a vantage point that can be seen from all over Newport.

St Woolos Pro-Cathedral c1945 N25116
The creation of the diocese of Monmouth in 1911 led to St Woolos being granted full cathedral status in 1949. This building has always been remarkable for its mixture of architectural styles, from its Saxon chapel to the Norman nave and the modern east end. Here, in the chancel, is the rose window, an abstract-design stained glass window golden with autumnal colours, which was designed by artist John Piper in 1964.

St Woolos Church, The Interior 1893 32633
We walk into the Norman nave, which is enhanced by two 15th-century aisles, through the impressive Norman arched doorway, whose stone columns were reputedly procured from the Roman remains at Caerleon. At the eastern end of the aisle is an elaborate wooden pulpit.

**St Mary's Church
1893** 32635
This Roman Catholic
church stands on Stow
Hill on the site of a
smaller Catholic chapel;
it was completed in
1840. Construction was
temporarily delayed
when the builders
downed tools to join the
Chartist marchers who
were travelling past on
their way to the
Westgate Hotel.

◄ **The Handpost Inn c1955** N25191
This public house, situated at the top of Stow Hill, is at a cross-roads, with Risca Road to the right and Baesleg Road to the left. This was once the primary road leading to Cardiff. It was built in 1873.

▼ **Christchurch and Church House c1955** N25142
The children's clothing and the style of the car are the only aspects of this scene to indicate that it is not the present day. The 12th century gave us the first documented evidence of a church on this site; over the years many changes have occurred, including reconstruction after a fire in 1949.

◄ **St Mark's Church c1955** N25195
Here we see an early Perpendicular-style church at Gold Tops; it opened in 1874. Running alongside it is Serpentine Road. At the turn of the 20th century, this was seen as one of the wealthier areas of Newport.

The Bridge 1893 32630
Looking over the railings of the bridge, we are able to make out
some of the town buildings. The clock tower of the Town Hall is on
the left, and the raised central column of the New Market is right of
centre. The brick building on the right was the Bridge Hotel, which
then later became the Shaftesbury Cafe.

The Castle 1893 32631
The castle was first built as a wooden structure in 1126. In 1402 Owain Glyndwr destroyed it and the bridge. During its lifetime, this castle has served as a tannery, a warehouse, a nail factory and, as we see here, the Searle-Herrings Brewery.

The Bridge and the Castle 1896 38698
Standing on the banks opposite the castle, we are able to observe the underbelly of Newport Bridge. This stone structure was built in 1800. Sixty-five years later, footpaths were added. In 1924 it was demolished to make way for the present crossing. A famous visitor to the bridge was Harry Houdini, who in 1913 as part of his act leaped from it in shackles to make a daring underwater escape.

**The Bridge
and the Castle 1903**
49482
Clarence Bridge, later
Newport Bridge, leads
us through the Old
Green Crossing and
into the High Street,
where we can see the
dome of the Corn
Exchange. To the right
is the Shaftesbury Cafe,
which in 1915 was to
become Jay's Furnishing
Stores before it was
demolished. Alongside
it is Bangor Wharf.

The Bridge and the Castle ▶
c1955 N25228

This photograph, taken from the Newport Motor Company, offers us a view of the sheer drop from the Castle down to the mud flats of the estuary. It was into the central tower, seen here on the right, where boats arriving with provisions for the castle entered at high tide. Over the castle walls you can make out the Castle Hotel, which has since been demolished, and behind that St Mark's church.

The Bridge c1955 N25203
In the distance is the turquoise dome of Newport Technical Institute, which opened in 1910 at a cost of £40,000. It is situated in Clarence Place, at this time opposite the Newport Motor Company. To the right is the sign for Davis Bros Ltd, who conducted their business from here until 1994, when Robert Price builder's merchants took over.

▼ **The Castle 1950** N25122
In the foreground we can see the centre of the old Green Crossing. To our left above the castle is the Great Western Railway bridge, with a train rattling across heading outward from Wales into England. Across Newport Bridge you can see pedestrians walking toward the Newport Motor Company, where now stands the Clarence House building, which dominates the skyline.

▼ **The Castle c1950** N25126
In this photograph we can see that the castle has been renovated somewhat. This restoration was begun in 1930 by the Ministry of Works. To this day the central tower contains an impressive vaulted ceiling. Notice on the left-hand side the number 3 bus on route from Malpas to its destination, Tradegar Park. In the background we see the green fields of Lodge Hill.

The Cenotaph 1925 ▲
77462 ▶
To commemorate the loss of Newport's servicemen in the Great War, the Cenotaph was erected in Clarence Place in 1923 and unveiled by Lord Tradegar. Here, two years after it was built, flowers and tributes are still laid at its base. In the background we can see the electric trams on route 4 travelling from the town centre via the bridge. The electric tramway opened in 1903.

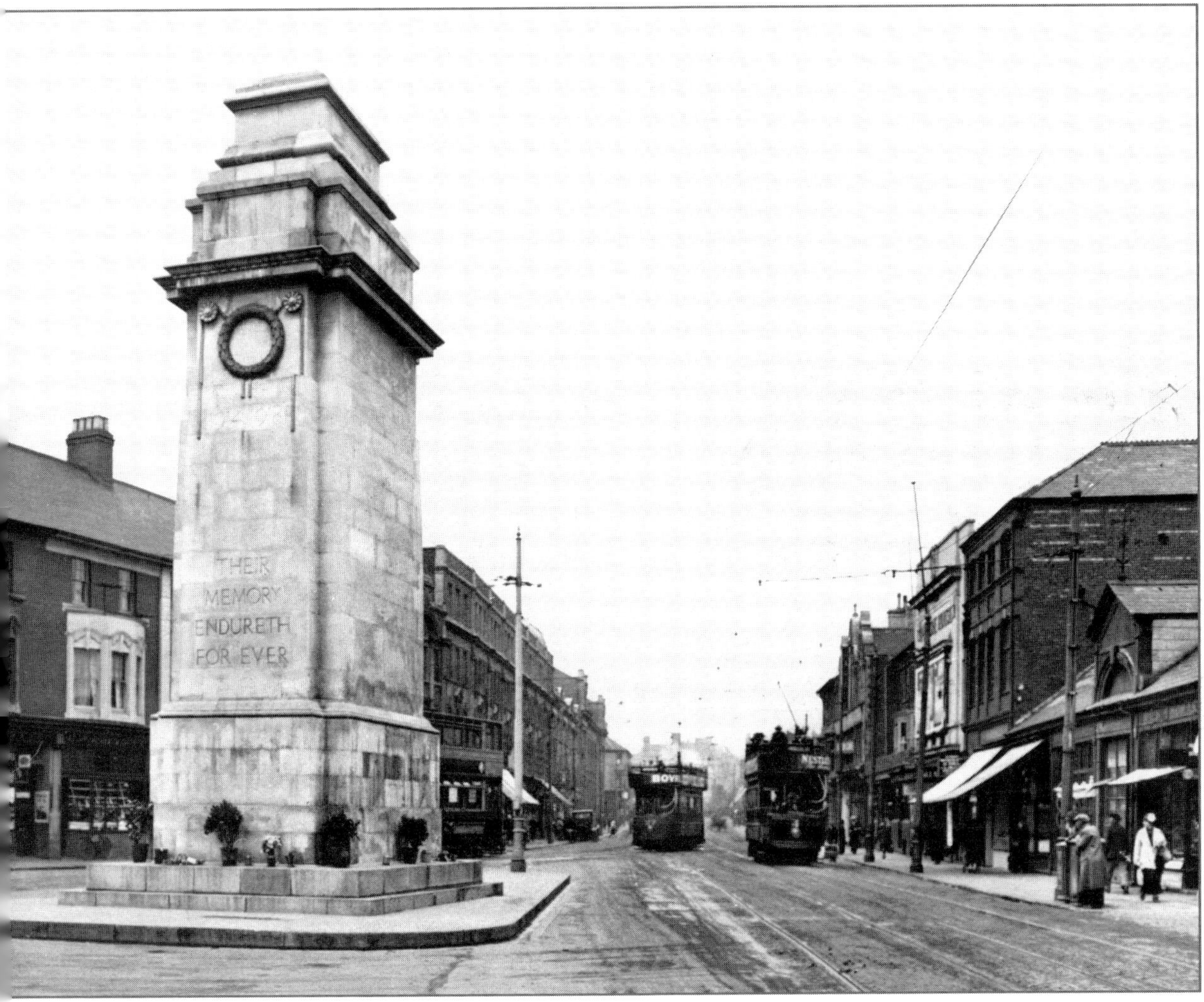
THEIR
MEMORY
ENDURETH
FOR EVER

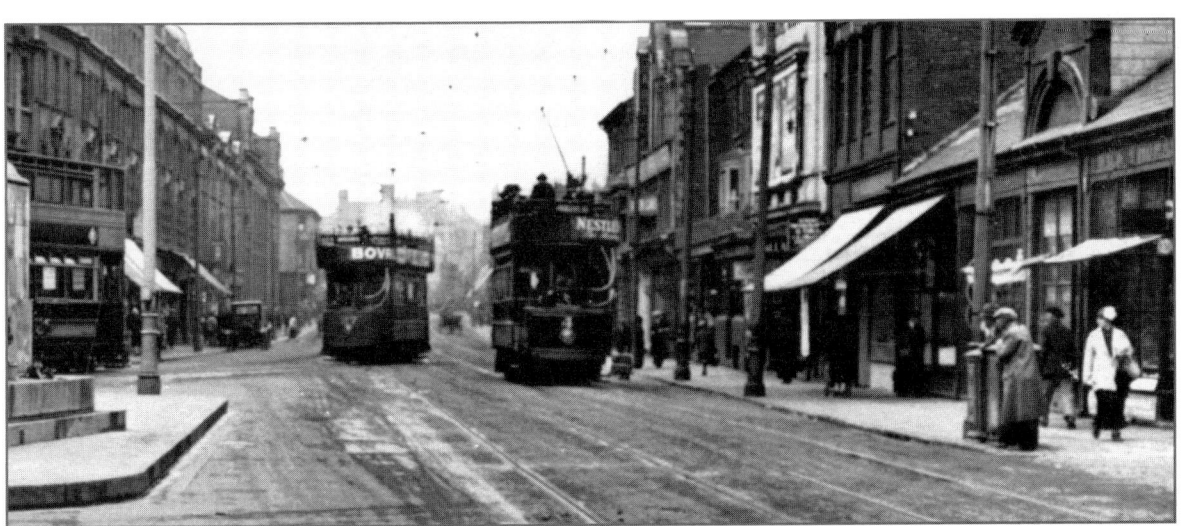

◀ The Cenotaph c1955
N25205

Crossing Newport Bridge into Clarence Place, we come directly to this war memorial. Tax offices have replaced the bed & breakfast and the funeral directors we see behind it. To the right amongst the shops and offices is Boots. Behind this is the building of the Liverpool Victoria Insurance Company; it is still standing today, although now it is a florist.

◄ The Cenotaph and Clarence Place c1950 N25124

Standing here in front of Albert E Hick's funeral directors, and looking toward the Cenotaph, we would have a clear view of Newport Bridge and beyond it Newport town centre. To the right of the memorial is the Odeon Cinema, with a Tyrone Power movie showing. This building still remains, and is now a snooker hall.

▼ The Vale of Usk from St Julians c1955 N25151

As we follow the winding road down into Caerleon, or Isca Silurum, as the Romans called their garrison town, we first encounter the St Julians pub. Proceeding on to pause before the stone bridge, completed in 1810, we encounter the Hanbury Arms Inn, built in c1565. This where Alfred Lord Tennyson reputedly sat 300 years later to write 'Idylls of the King'.

◄ Caerleon, The Village 1893 32643

In front of us is Ashwell House. We can enjoy this view today from the Kings Arms on Bellmont Hill. The road curving away from us leads across the stone bridge into Caerleon village. In the distance is Lodge Hill. The University of Wales College, Newport, is situated on Lodge Road.

Caerleon, The Bridge c1955 C4017
This stone bridge was constructed in 1810, replacing an earlier wooden structure. Along the right-hand side of the bank you can make out brick remains: this was once a well-used wharf, which dealt in the transfer of passengers and goods. Out of shot on the left-hand side is the Ship Inn, and beyond that the Hanbury Arms.

Caerleon, The Village 1899 43660
Positioned in the centre of this photograph is the Bull Inn; as its sign says, it benefited from good stabling. Next door but one is the grocers shop of G F Thorne. Notice the promotions on the facade: advertising is not a 20th-century phenomenon. Observe how free of traffic the village is.

Caerleon
The Square and the
War Memorial c1930
C4020

Caerleon's District War Memorial, unveiled in May 1921, dominates this scene. The bronze inlays contain the names of those soldiers who fell in the Great War; it also acts as a water fountain. Behind them is Berrys Drapery and Stationary store. Perhaps the girls outside are waiting for it to open. Parked out in front is an old Ford model-T car, which might have belonged to the shop's owners, Mr and Mrs P Berry.

Caerleon
The Museum and the Church 1899 43654
The Museum of Roman Antiquities, now called the Roman Legionary Museum, opened in 1850. Opening admission prices were 3d for adults and 1d for children. Beyond the trees we can make out the tower of St Cadoc's Church, which dates from Norman times. Its clock was installed twelve years before this photograph was taken to commemorate the Golden Jubilee of Queen Victoria.

Caerleon
The Roman Arch 1931 C4023
This is not the work of Roman architects, but the folly of a Miss Elizabeth Morgan, who had it built in 1820 using stone reclaimed from the remains of Roman buildings. The Priory that we glimpse through the arch was built in about 1179, and at present is a hotel.

Caerleon
Station Approach 1910 62523
We are standing here on Station Road looking towards Ponthir. To the left we can see the window display of a general store, a vast array of bottles and boxed goods. Across the road is a sign for Tom Herbert Coal Merchant. On the deserted road a group of children come toward us; the eldest a boy in a peaked cap pushes his youngest sibling in a perambulator.

▲ **The Civic Centre c1950** N25188
Overlooking the central area of Newport is this grandiose building. Designed by Mr Howitt, it
was endorsed by His Majesty King George VI and his bride Queen Elizabeth in 1937, when he
cut the first sod of earth. The silver spade he used is now part of Newport Museum's collection.

The Architecture of the Town Centre

▲ **The Law Courts and Civic Centre c1950** N25138

Construction of this building was halted in 1939 owing to the outbreak of the Second World War. The Admiralty used sections of the unfinished centre for storage. The council chamber was finally finished in 1956, and eight years later an entrance hall, a marble staircase and a clocktower were added. The most impressive and decorative aspect of the Civic Centre is the collection of giant murals by Hans Feibusch.

High Street 1893

32627

The Corn Exchange on the Old Green is visible in the distance. The National Provincial Bank is on the left and Gloucester Bank Chambers is on the right. A guard stands at the entrance. The building opposite with three awnings is now a red and yellow-fronted McDonalds.

High Street 1896

38696

Horse-drawn vehicles
run along the High
Street. Groups of
pedestrians stand
together and talk over
the problems of the day.
Women are dressed in
corsets and gowns, and
men are wearing bowler
hats and flat caps.
Notice the awnings over
the shop fronts
shielding the windows
against the sun.

High Street 1903 49481a
In front of us are the Savoy buildings, complete with a restaurant, and adjoining it is the Post Office. On the right of the picture is the Corn Exchange, built in 1878 as a tribute to Lord Tredegar's services to agriculture and farming.

High Street 1910 62509
Flanking the High Street are the Bank of England and the United Counties Bank. Notice the electric tram at the centre of the photograph. Newport's electric tramway was opened in 1903; it was replaced in 1937 by the motor bus services.

Extracts from: **High Street 1910** 62509 **& High Street 1903** 49481a (see previous page)

Savoy Buildings 1910
62512
The full expanse of the Post Office and the Savoy Hotel and Grill is illustrated in this photograph. In 1913 the latter was acquired as part of the new post office development. In the foreground, to the left you can see an ices sign on the Murenger House; its facade is much plainer at this time than the striking black and white Tudor style seen in the c1950 photograph.

High Street 1910
62510
Here we stand at the Old Green, now a very busy roundabout, looking toward Clarence Place, with the dome of the technical college on the right. In the foreground is the Shaftesbury Temperance Hotel. Opposite are shop fronts, including a sign for E Hill's Shoeing and General Forge.

◄ High Street c1950
N25183
The left-hand side of High Street boasts Lovell's Restaurant, Dunn and Co Tailors and the Greyhound Hotel, now just a public house. The Greyhound was the setting for the formation of Newport Harriers running club in 1896. In 1984 one of its members, Steve Jones, became a world record holder after winning the Chicago Marathon.

◀ High Street c1950 N25201

In the distance is the new Post Office building, which was demolished to make way for the present development of offices, a coffee-house and a club. The facades above the shops at the top end of the High Street have changed very little in the last century. The building on the left is still a bank, now Nat West, and Noel Fashions on Skinner Street has become the Principality.

▼ High Street c1950
N25184

We are given a clear view of Stow Hill in this image. To the right, the Clock Tower is perched at the apex of the Bank Building. The three stone columns belong to the National Provincial Bank of England - notice the Union Jack fluttering at the top of the flagpole. Left of the photograph are the many windows of the Westgate Hotel.

◀ High Street and the General Post Office c1950 N25127

This area has undergone a great deal of development in the past couple of years. The Post Office building in the foreground, built in 1855, has been transformed into car parking and office block facilities. The facade has been maintained and restored. The buildings beyond were demolished in 1980 as part of a ring road development.

The New Market
High Street c1950 N25140
On the right is the market building, re-built in 1889;
there has probably been a market of sorts on this
site since the 16th century. In the distance is the
station approach and the Great Western Railway
station, opened in 1930. The busy streets here
reflect today's commercial pedestrian traffic.

Ye Olde Murenger House c1950 N25139

It is believed that this three-storied Tudor building dates back to the 14th century, although it can only be positively traced back to 1541. Its name is the cause of much contention. Some maintain that it acquired its name from an officer who might have lived here employed to collect the 'murenger'(murengers were tolls used to maintain the town wall). The facade of this house has changed over the years; it has undergone extensive repairs, and nearly collapsed in the 1980s. It is now a listed building, and Newport's oldest public house.

Commercial Street 1901 47897
A policeman patrols the street, glancing into Baker's Boots. On the opposite side is the drapers W Smith; next to that is the Lord Raglan, offering wines, spirits and a game of billiards. In the distance is a tram heading toward Westgate Square and High Street.

Extracts from: **Commercial Street 1901** 47897 (see previous page)

Commercial Street 1893 32629
Once again we see the Town Hall monopolising our view. It was opened in
1885, and designed by the architects T M Lockwood and E A Landsdowne.
Now demolished, it is the site of British Home Stores.

Commercial Street 1901 47896
Here we see Newman and Sons selling pianos, while next door is Lipton the grocers. Opposite is the Westgate, where in 1839 the Chartists' marches gathered after walking from Blackwood, Nantyglo and Pontypool. A riot ensued, and over 20 lost their lives. Bullet holes can still be found inside the Westgate. Now under refurbishment to become part of a shopping complex, its facade is to remain intact.

▼ **Commercial Street 1903** 49479
This aerial view allows us to look down on the open-top electric tram with a passenger just boarding. Considering that this is a main shopping street, we notice that there are very few pedestrians. In the distance is the Town Hall with its clock tower, and to the right is the Westgate Hotel.

▼ **Westgate Square, Commercial Street and the Town Hall c1948** N25112
The Royal London Insurance Society is on our immediate left; it is now a mobile phone shop, a sign of the times, perhaps. The commercial premises at the base of the Westgate Hotel are a hive of activity. By this stage electric trams had been replaced by a motor bus service, although here you can still see the tramlines and wires. This is now a pedestrianised area.

▲ **Commercial Street and the Town Hall Tower c1950** N25141
1986 saw the complete pedestrianisation of Commercial Street; here it is bustling with traffic and pedestrians. Two motor buses can be seen: the foremost bus shows its destination as Westgate. In the background on the left is Barclays Bank, just as it is today.

◄ Commercial Street 1901
47899

The church here on the right has long since been demolished; next to it is the domed building that is now Lloyds Bank. Further in the distance is the tower of the Town Hall. In the foreground a young boy in period clothes looks toward the camera; notice his starched white collar.

**Commercial Street
1910** 62511
We see here intense
advertising from
Wildings Limited,
Clothiers. This building
is now utilised by
Clark's Shoes. Wildings
department store still
has a place on the
opposite side of
Commercial Street. The
hotel on the left is now
the Body Shop.

Commercial Street 1901 47898
A beautiful Victorian street lamp dominates this scene. Rising above the rooftops is the spire of St Paul's church, opened in 1836; it is still here today and undergoing refurbishment. The horse-drawn tram in front of us boasts signs for Lipton's Teas and Milkmaid milk. From the signs above the shop fronts, we can see that the tram is passing E Cauffman and Scaplehorn, a saddler and harness maker.

Royal Gwent Hospital 1901 47900
Walking down Commercial Street onto Cardiff Road, we come to what was the Newport and Monmouthshire
Hospital; it was opened the year this photograph was taken by the Right Hon Viscount Tredegar. Later, in 1913,
it become the Royal Gwent Hospital.

George Street Bridge c1965 N25251
This view of the bridge from Corporation Road allows us to view the expanse of this curved structure. It was
opened on 9 April 1964, and its connecting roads were completed two years later. The Ford Prefect car in the
foreground is following the flow of traffic across to Cardiff Road.

The Fabric of Industry

Traffic & Transport

Allt-yr-yn, Little Switzerland c1955 A38143
This viewing point from Ridgeway has not altered at all in the past forty-five years. To the right is the reservoir, and to the left are the steps of the Fourteen Locks. Over the horizon are Risca and Cwmbran.

▼ **Allt-yr-yn, Little Switzerland c1955** A38146
Twmbarllum Mountain is the highest point in the distance. The cottage alongside the lock exists still, and the dog kennels is in business here.

▼ **Allt-yr-yn, The Canal c1955** A38144
Two boys walk over the stone bridge past the farmhouse, still there alongside the beauty of the canal. This section is on the stretch approaching the Fourteen Locks. Refurbishment of Newport's canals began in 1980.

▲ **Allt-yr-yn On the Canal 1893**
32641
The Monmouthshire and Brecon canal was constructed in 1792, and was officially opened in 1799. The engineer was Thomas Dadford. Here, on this quiet stretch of water, two fisherman wait patiently for a bite on their line.

**Allt-yr-yn, On the Canal
1893** 32639
A main line of the canal was
authorised by the
government in 1792. It
stretched from Newport
to Pontnewynydd, with a
branch from Crumlin to
Malpas twelve miles long.
This gave Newport the
ability to transport coal and
iron to her docks for export.

On the Canal 1896 ▶
38708

Here we look toward the Fourteen Locks and Crumlin, where an information centre and picnic area is now established. Just over thirty years after this photograph was taken, the last commercial traffic to pay tolls travelled on the main section of Newport's canals.

▼ **On the Canal 1896**
38706

This stretch of the Monmouthshire and Brecon canal lies between Bettws and Malpas. Malpas is derived from Norman French and means 'the bad pass'. By this date the railways had started to take over from the barges as transporters of Newport's industrial goods.

▲ **On the Canal Fourteen Locks 1896**
38707

This is the highest point of the Monmouthshire Canal; here it makes its way over 'Little Switzerland' to Crumlin. The Welsh prophet Merlin predicted that here a river would flow over the mountain and that ships would travel upon it.

◀ Allt-yr-yn
Above the Lock 1893
32637
The path running parallel to the canal, seen here in the top right-hand corner of the photograph, is still there, but is now slightly overgrown. Here the canal is peaceful, free of pedestrians and of cargo-laden barges.

▼ Allt-yr-yn, The Village 1893 32636

Twmbarllum in the distance watches over the houses of Allt-yr-yn and the farmer's fields laden with crops. There is a large pond behind the white house that is there still. Another attraction in this area was a lido.

▼ Town Reach 1893 32623

This area is now under development; the brick building on the left-hand side of the photograph is at present a restaurant. The land running alongside it has been cleared of buildings and is waiting for the construction of an arts centre. Along the riverbank is situated the 'Steel Wave', Peter Fink's 1990 giant sculpture.

▲ The Docks South Quay c1955

N25179

The Town Dock was opened in 1842, followed by the Alexandra Dock in 1875 and the South Alexandra in 1893. The ship anchored here is named the 'Clan Maclay'. A motto was displayed throughout the town after the launch of the new docks: 'May the lock of Newport Dock be opened by the keys of the commercial world'.

◀ **View from the Transporter Bridge c1950**
N25157
The walkway of the bridge allows us to admire a panoramic view of Alexandra Docks and the residential houses of Pillgwenly. If we look to the base of the structure, directly behind it we can see the West of England public house.

The Transporter Bridge 1910 62513
Here we see the bridge-house poised on the bank of the Usk. Attendants wait in readiness at the gate for
passengers wanting to travel to the east side of the river. Notice the platform at the top of the photograph where
pedestrians, if brave enough, are able to walk across 242 ft above the ground.

The Transporter Bridge 1906 54935A
This photograph was taken the year the bridge opened. The cradle is in movement, transporting pedestrians and cars high across the Usk, thus preventing any disruption to the shipping channel. The platform is capable of carrying six vehicles and 100 passengers. In the foreground is a paddle steamer. These still work out of Newport Dock, taking day-trippers to destinations such as Weston and Clevedon.

The Transporter Bridge 1906 N25036
The bridge was designed by the engineers R H Haynes of Newport and the Frenchman F Arnodin, at a cost of £98,000. The bridge is shown here in all her glory; the impressive span is 645 ft. In 1958 it was used in the making of the film 'Tiger Bay' starring Hayley Mills.

Newport's Exterior & Boundaries and Beyond

Belle Vue Park 1910 62515

Belle Vue Park 1925 77456
Relaxed summer visitors recline on the terraces
of the greenhouse buildings. The grand stone
staircase leads downward to the densely-seated area
encircling the bandstand. Sunday concerts are still
held here with a rebuilt bandstand. Tennis matches
and bowling tournaments were also enjoyed within
these grounds. Belle Vue also boasted a small zoo,
including peacocks and monkeys.

▼ **Belle Vue Park 1896** 38704
This photograph was taken two years after the park was opened. Emerging through the trees we can see the bandstand, and behind it the greenhouses. These were used to cultivate the flowers that were displayed throughout Newport's parks. Today only the basic structure remains. Music and culture further enhanced Belle Vue when in 1897 the Welsh National Eisteddfod was held here.

▼ **Belle Vue Park c1945** N25119
The sloping outskirts of the park offer a perfect opportunity for the Sunday visitor to admire the imposing structure of the transporter bridge and the residential homes of Pillgwenlly that surround it. At the bottom of the park, children are entertained in the playground. Originally this land was called 'Round Table Field', alluding to the myth that it was once the meeting place of King Arthur and his knights.

▲ **The Lighthouse 1910**
62517
The West Usk Lighthouse, St Brides, was built in 1821 and designed by James Walker. Thirteen years after this photograph was taken it was sold for private use. During the 20th century, it has proved a popular destination for day-trippers.

◄ **Cwmbran**
General View c1955
C547009
W H Davies wrote in his poem 'The Mind's Liberty' about the mountain we see here on the horizon: 'Twm Barlum, that green pap in Gwent With its dark nipple in a cloud'.

**Cwmbran
Victoria Street c1955**
C547014
The appearance of this street has changed little in forty-five years. The National Provincial Bank is at present a security firm. To the right is the County Constabulary, built in 1898, now the Council House. The memorial clock tower standing guard at the centre of the road was erected in February 1936 to commemorate those soldiers who gave their lives in the First World War.

▼ Llantarnam, St Michael and All Angels' Church c1955 L548073

This Norman building is the parish church of Llantarnam; it is thought to have been used originally by the Cistercians. Outside its main door is a cross: its upper half is probably 18th-century, and the lower half medieval. The interior includes a chancel with a chapel, a nave and south porch.

▼ Pontymister, The Canal Bridge and Mariah Hill c1955 P309006

This peaceful stretch of canal leads us to the Prince of Wales public house. Stone-built Mariah Bridge on the right leads to Rosemont Avenue. Fishermen are still to be seen here casting their rods into the canal waters.

▲ Pontymister Commercial Street c1955 P309009

This street has changed very little since the 1950s. On the right, out of shot, is the Salvation Army; on the same side of the road just past the telegraph pole is the Commercial pub. Notice the pylons in a period before cables were laid underground out of sight.

◄ **Pontymister
Ty-Isaf c1955** P309003
The winding road in front
of us is called Channel View;
beneath it are the railway
lines, now reduced to one
main line. This is primarily
used to transport coils from
Llanwern Steel Works to
Ebbw Vale Steel Works for
further processing.

Bassaleg
The Post Office c1955
B670006
Washing powder and
Windolene
advertisements adorn
the Post Office walls.
A young boy in a school
cap leaves the store,
probably with sweets. At
the bottom of the road is
the T A public house,
and beyond that we look
towards the Gaer.

Cwmcarn, General View c1950 C548014
The railway bridge in the background is known as the Long Bridge, or Black Bridge, and replaced an earlier structure built by Benjamin Hall. The large building to the right of the picture was the Miners Institute, and is now a library. Sandwiched between the rows of houses in the top right of the photograph is the railway line to Cwmcarn. Below is a memorial park honouring the bravery of servicemen from the two world wars.

Cwmcarn, Newport Road c1950 C548005
In the foreground we can see the shop front of the Cwmbran Post Office exhibiting an elaborate book display - the post office is open for business to this day. A short walk along the street brings us to Jack Hatfield's Cycle Shop, replaced now by physiotherapists. Across the street is the Park Hall cinema.

Risca
General View c1965 R328041
To the left are the smoking chimneys of Pontymister Steel Works,
which have since been demolished. The flat green fields in the
centre of the town are called the Risca Welfare and Bowling Green.
Through the trees we can see Channel View.

Risca, Tredegar Street c1965 R328081
Nearly out of shot is the façade of the Mariah Baptist Church. Across the road is the white-fronted Lloyds Bank, now a computer store. The row of shops opposite are utilised by Spar and Kwiksave. The Gas store has gone.

Risca, Tredegar Street c1955 R328018
Walking along this street, we encounter Cloughs Cleaners, with the library next door. Further along, and in between residential houses, is Boots the Chemists with an elaborate window display. Barclays Bank is still positioned here.

Index

Frith Book Co Titles

www.frithbook.co.uk

The Frith Book Company publishes over 100 new titles each year. A selection of those currently available are listed below. For latest catalogue please contact Frith Book Co.

Town Books 96pp, 100 photos. County and Themed Books 128pp, 150 photos (unless specified). All titles hardback laminated case and jacket except those indicated pb (paperback)

Around Aylesbury (pb)	1-85937-227-9	£9.99	Down the Thames	1-85937-121-3	£14.99
Around Bakewell	1-85937-113-2	£12.99	Around Dublin	1-85937-058-6	£12.99
Around Barnstaple	1-85937-084-5	£12.99	Around Dublin (pb)	1-85937-	£9.99
Around Bath	1-85937-097-7	£12.99	East Anglia (pb)	1-85937-265-1	£9.99
Berkshire (pb)	1-85937-191-4	£9.99	East London	1-85937-080-2	£14.99
Around Blackpool	1-85937-049-7	£12.99	East Sussex	1-85937-130-2	£14.99
Around Bognor Regis	1-85937-055-1	£12.99	Around Eastbourne	1-85937-061-6	£12.99
Around Bournemouth	1-85937-067-5	£12.99	Edinburgh (pb)	1-85937-193-0	£8.99
Around Bradford (pb)	1-85937-204-x	£9.99	English Castles	1-85937-078-0	£14.99
Brighton (pb)	1-85937-192-2	£8.99	English Country Houses	1-85937-161-2	£17.99
British Life A Century Ago	1-85937-103-5	£17.99	Around Exeter	1-85937-126-4	£12.99
British Life A Century Ago (pb)	1-85937-213-9	£9.99	Exmoor	1-85937-132-9	£14.99
Buckinghamshire (pb)	1-85937-200-7	£9.99	Around Falmouth	1-85937-066-7	£12.99
Camberley (pb)	1-85937-222-8	£9.99	Folkestone	1-85937-124-8	£9.99
Around Cambridge	1-85937-092-6	£12.99	Gloucestershire	1-85937-102-7	£14.99
Cambridgeshire	1-85937-086-1	£14.99	Around Great Yarmouth	1-85937-085-3	£12.99
Canals and Waterways	1-85937-129-9	£17.99	Greater Manchester (pb)	1-85937-266-x	£9.99
Cardiff (pb)	1-85937-093-4	£9.99	Around Guildford	1-85937-117-5	£12.99
Carmarthenshire	1-85937-216-3	£14.99	Around Harrogate	1-85937-112-4	£12.99
Cheltenham (pb)	1-85937-095-0	£9.99	Hastings & Bexhill (pb)	1-85937-131-0	£9.99
Around Chester	1-85937-090-x	£12.99	Helston (pb)	1-85937-214-7	£9.99
Around Chichester	1-85937-089-6	£12.99	Herefordshire	1-85937-174-4	£14.99
Around Chichester (pb)	1-85937-228-7	£9.99	Around Horsham	1-85937-127-2	£12.99
Churches of Berkshire	1-85937-170-1	£17.99	Humberside	1-85937-215-5	£14.99
Churches of Dorset	1-85937-172-8	£17.99	Around Ipswich	1-85937-133-7	£12.99
Colchester (pb)	1-85937-188-4	£8.99	Ireland (pb)	1-85937-181-7	£9.99
Cornish Coast	1-85937-163-9	£14.99	Isle of Man	1-85937-065-9	£14.99
Cornwall	1-85937-054-3	£14.99	Isle of Wight	1-85937-114-0	£14.99
Cornwall (pb)	1-85937-229-5	£9.99	Kent (pb)	1-85937-189-2	£9.99
Cotswolds (pb)	1-85937-	£9.99	Kent Living Memories	1-85937-125-6	£14.99
County Durham	1-85937-123-x	£14.99	Lancaster, Morecambe & Heysham (pb)		
Cumbria	1-85937-101-9	£14.99		1-85937-233-3	£9.99
Dartmoor	1-85937-145-0	£14.99	Leeds (pb)	1-85937-202-3	£9.99
Derbyshire (pb)	1-85937-196-5	£9.99	Around Leicester	1-85937-073-x	£12.99
Devon	1-85937-052-7	£14.99	Leicestershire (pb)	1-85937-185-x	£9.99
Dorset	1-85937-075-6	£14.99	Around Lincoln	1-85937-111-6	£12.99
Dorset Coast	1-85937-062-4	£14.99	Lincolnshire	1-85937-135-3	£14.99
Dorset Living Memories	1-85937-210-4	£14.99	London (pb)	1-85937-183-3	£9.99
Down the Severn	1-85937-118-3	£14.99	Ludlow (pb)	1-85937-176-0	£9.99

Available from your local bookshop or from the publisher

Frith Book Co Titles (continued)

Around Maidstone	1-85937-056-x	£12.99	South Devon Living Memories	1-85937-168-x	£14.99
Manchester (pb)	1-85937-198-1	£9.99	Staffordshire (96pp)	1-85937-047-0	£12.99
Peterborough (pb)	1-85937-219-8	£9.99	Stone Circles & Ancient Monuments		
Piers	1-85937-237-6	£17.99		1-85937-143-4	£17.99
New Forest	1-85937-128-0	£14.99	Around Stratford upon Avon	1-85937-098-5	£12.99
Around Newark	1-85937-105-1	£12.99	Suffolk (pb)	1-85937-221-x	£9.99
Around Newquay	1-85937-140-x	£12.99	Surrey (pb)	1-85937-	
Norfolk (pb)	1-85937-195-7	£9.99	Sussex (pb)	1-85937-184-1	£9.99
North Devon Coast	1-85937-146-9	£14.99	Swansea (pb)	1-85937-167-1	£9.99
North Yorks	1-85937-236-8	£9.99	Tees Valley & Cleveland	1-85937-211-2	£14.99
Norwich (pb)	1-85937-194-9	£8.99	Thanet (pb)	1-85937-116-7	£9.99
Around Nottingham	1-85937-060-8	£12.99	Tiverton (pb)	1-85937-178-7	£9.99
Nottinghamshire (pb)	1-85937-187-6	£9.99	Around Torbay	1-85937-063-2	£12.99
Around Oxford	1-85937-096-9	£12.99	Around Truro	1-85937-147-7	£12.99
Peak District	1-85937-100-0	£14.99	Victorian & Edwardian Kent	1-85937-149-3	£14.99
Around Penzance	1-85937-069-1	£12.99	Victorian & Edwardian Maritime Album		
Around Plymouth	1-85937-119-1	£12.99		1-85937-144-2	£17.99
Norfolk Living Memories	1-85937-217-1	£14.99	Victorian and Edwardian Sussex		
North Yorks (pb)	1-85937-236-8	£9.99		1-85937-157-4	£14.99
Preston (pb)	1-85937-212-0	£9.99	Victorian & Edwardian Yorkshire	1-85937-154-x	£14.99
Reading (pb)	1-85937-238-4	£9.99	Victorian Seaside	1-85937-159-0	£17.99
Salisbury (pb)	1-85937-239-2	£9.99	Warwickshire (pb)	1-85937-203-1	£9.99
Around St Ives	1-85937-068-3	£12.99	West Midlands	1-85937-109-4	£14.99
Around Scarborough	1-85937-104-3	£12.99	West Sussex	1-85937-148-5	£14.99
Scotland (pb)	1-85937-182-5	£9.99	West Yorkshire (pb)	1-85937-201-5	£9.99
Around Sevenoaks and Tonbridge	1-85937-057-8	£12.99	Weymouth (pb)	1-85937-209-0	£9.99
Somerset	1-85937-153-1	£14.99	Wiltshire Living Memories	1-85937-245-7	£14.99
South Hams	1-85937-220-1	£14.99	Around Winchester	1-85937-139-6	£12.99
Around Southampton	1-85937-088-8	£12.99	Windmills & Watermills	1-85937-242-2	£17.99
Around Southport	1-85937-106-x	£12.99	Worcestershire	1-85937-152-3	£14.99
Around Shrewsbury	1-85937-110-8	£12.99	York (pb)	1-85937-199-x	£9.99
Shropshire	1-85937-083-7	£14.99	Yorkshire Living Memories	1-85937-166-3	£14.99
South Devon Coast	1-85937-107-8	£14.99			

Frith Book Co titles available 2001

Lake District (pb)	1-85937-275-9	£9.99	Luton (pb)	1-85937-235-x	£9.99
Sussex (pb)	1-85937-184-1	£9.99	Cheshire (pb)	1-85937-271-6	£9.99
Northumberland and Tyne & Wear (pb)			Peak District (pb)	1-85937-280-5	£9.99
	1-85937-281-3	£9.99	Dorset (pb)	1-85937-269-4	£9.99
Devon (pb)	1-85937-297-x	£9.99	Liverpool and Merseyside (pb)	1-85937-234-1	£9.99
Bedford (pb)	1-85937-205-8	£9.99	Surrey (pb)	1-85937-081-0	£9.99
Down the Thames (pb)	1-85937-278-3	£9.99	Buckinghamshire (pb)	1-85937-200-7	£9.99
Hereford (pb)	1-85937-175-2	£9.99	Heart of Lancashire (pb)	1-85937-197-3	£9.99
Brighton (pb)	1-85937-192-2	£9.99			

See Frith books on the internet www.frithbook.co.uk

FRITH PRODUCTS & SERVICES

Francis Frith would doubtless be pleased to know that the pioneering publishing venture he started in 1860 still continues today. A hundred and forty years later, The Francis Frith Collection continues in the same innovative tradition and is now one of the foremost publishers of vintage photographs in the world. Some of the current activities include:

Interior Decoration

Today Frith's photographs can be seen framed and as giant wall murals in thousands of pubs, restaurants, hotels, banks, retail stores and other public buildings throughout the country. In every case they enhance the unique local atmosphere of the places they depict and provide reminders of gentler days in an increasingly busy and frenetic world.

Product Promotions

Frith products are used by many major companies to promote the sales of their own products or to reinforce their own history and heritage. Frith promotions have been used by Hovis bread, Courage beers, Scots Porage Oats, Colman's mustard, Cadbury's foods, Mellow Birds coffee, Dunhill pipe tobacco, Guinness, and Bulmer's Cider.

Genealogy and Family History

As the interest in family history and roots grows world-wide, more and more people are turning to Frith's photographs of Great Britain for images of the towns, villages and streets where their ancestors lived; and, of course, photographs of the churches and chapels where their ancestors were christened, married and buried are an essential part of every genealogy tree and family album.

Frith Products

All Frith photographs are available Framed or just as Mounted Prints and Posters (size 23 x 16 inches). These may be ordered from the address below. From time to time other products - Address Books, Calendars, Table Mats, etc - are available.

The Internet

Already twenty thousand Frith photographs can be viewed and purchased on the internet. By the end of the year 2000 some 60,000 Frith photographs will be available on the internet. The number of sites is constantly expanding, each focussing on different products and services from the Collection.
The main Frith sites are listed below.
www.francisfrith.co.uk
www.frithbook.co.uk

See the complete list of Frith Books at:
www.frithbook.co.uk
This web site is regularly updated with the latest list of publications from the Frith Book Company. If you wish to buy books relating to another part of the country that your local bookshop does not stock, you may purchase on-line.

For further information, trade, or author enquiries please contact us at the address below:
The Francis Frith Collection, Frith's Barn, Teffont, Salisbury, Wiltshire, England SP3 5QP.
Tel: +44 (0)1722 716 376 Fax: +44 (0)1722 716 881 Email: sales@francisfrith.co.uk

---

See Frith books on the internet www.frithbook.co.uk

TO RECEIVE YOUR FREE MOUNTED PRINT

Mounted Print
Overall size 14 x 11 inches

Cut out this Voucher and return it with your remittance for £1.50 to cover postage and handling, to UK addresses. For overseas addresses please include £4.00 post and handling. Choose any photograph included in this book. Your SEPIA print will be A4 in size, and mounted in a cream mount with burgundy rule lines, overall size 14 x 11 inches.

Order additional Mounted Prints at HALF PRICE (only £7.49 each*)

If there are further pictures you would like to order, possibly as gifts for friends and family, purchase them at half price (no additional postage and handling required).

Have your Mounted Prints framed*

For an additional £14.95 per print you can have your chosen Mounted Print framed in an elegant polished wood and gilt moulding, overall size 16 x 13 inches (no additional postage and handling required).

---

* IMPORTANT!
These special prices are only available if ordered using the original voucher on this page (no copies permitted) and at the same time as your free Mounted Print, for delivery to the same address

---

Frith Collectors' Guild

From time to time we publish a magazine of news and stories about Frith photographs and further special offers of Frith products. If you would like 12 months FREE membership, please return this form.

Send completed forms to:
The Francis Frith Collection, Frith's Barn, Teffont, Salisbury, Wiltshire SP3 5QP

Voucher for FREE and Reduced Price Frith Prints

Picture no.	Page number	Qty	Mounted @ £7.49	Framed + £14.95	Total Cost
		1	**Free of charge***	£	£
			£7.49	£	£
			£7.49	£	£
			£7.49	£	£
			£7.49	£	£
			£7.49	£	£

Please allow 28 days for delivery *** Post & handling** **£1.50**

Book Title . . . . **Total Order Cost** **£**

Please do not photocopy this voucher. Only the original is valid, so please cut it out and return it to us.

I enclose a cheque / postal order for £ . . . . made payable to 'The Francis Frith Collection' OR please debit my Mastercard / Visa / Switch / Amex card *(credit cards please on all overseas orders)*

Number . . . .

Issue No(Switch only) . . . . .Valid from (Amex/Switch) . . . .

Expires . . . . Signature . . . .

Name Mr/Mrs/Ms . . . .

Address . . . .

. . . .

. . . . Postcode . . . .

Daytime Tel No . . . . Valid to 31/12/02

The Francis Frith Collectors' Guild

Please enrol me as a member for 12 months free of charge.

Name Mr/Mrs/Ms . . . .

Address . . . .

. . . .

. . . .

. . . . Postcode . . . .

Free Print - see overleaf